Horses

HORSES

Horses
in the
Animal World

Majestic horses roam freely in the wild of the Namib Desert. These once domesticated animals only rediscovered their freedom around 1900.

The evolution of the horse

The horse, ass, zebra, rhinoceros and tapir are all related. They can all legitimately lay claim to common ancestry, even if, today, the Equidae form a family on their own in which only the zebra and several types of ass can still be classed as wild.

Przewalski's horses, or the horses of the Gobi Desert, are the last remaining 'true' wild horses. These original horses have never been domesticated.

More than 40 million years of evolution have changed the anatomy of the horse, increasing the speed at which it can run.

It is true to say that we know more about the origins and evolution of the horse than any other animal. The many fossils that have been found in America and Asia have enabled us to build up a precise picture of its amazing development.

An even or odd number of toes

At first sight, it is tempting to group the horse with the cow and pig in the

The zebra, a close relative of the horse, has highly distinctive markings.

larger family of farm animals. The true ancestry of man's 'proudest conquest', however, lies with that of the pachydermal rhinoceros and the curious tapir. By way of proof, simply count the number of digits (or toes) that these animals have. The horse, rhinoceros and tapir all have an odd number of digits on each foot. For this reason they are grouped together under the order of Perissodactyla, whilst those animals with an even number of digits (cows, pigs...)

The rhinoceros still moves in a way that is similar to that of its cousin, the horse.

The small family of perissodactyl ungulates which includes the Equidae and rhinoceros also numbers a rather strange individual: the tapir.

are classed as artiodactyls. The one similarity that links these two groups is the fact that they are all ungulates that walk on their nails which have become hooves. The honour of being the father of all Equidae goes to *Hyracotherium*. Fossilized remains prove that it is without a doubt the common ancestor of the horse, the ass and the zebra.

A slow evolution

There was, however, nothing horse-like about *Hyracotherium*. Living mainly in Eurasia, it was not much bigger than a dog and had four digits on each of its front feet and three on each of those at the back. An inhabitant of the tropical jungle that covered the area at that time, *Hyracotherium* was severely affected by the first glacial periods and was finally wiped out over 40 million years ago. Its American cousin, *Eohippus*, had a little more luck. This small speckled animal survived the rigours of evolution for another 30 million years, developing into *Mesohippus*, *Miohippus* and finally *Merychippus*, each species adapting more or less to the massive changes taking place on the planet.

Years of evolution have transformed the horse into a machine designed to run.

The father of all Equidae is *Hyracotherium*.

▼ During the prehistoric period, nature seems to have let its imagination run riot and many perissodactyls, such as the present horse, rhinoceros and tapir, were created in a variety of incredible shapes and sizes. Some 35 million years ago, an animal looking rather like a gigantic horse measuring five metres high and seven long gambolled carelessly through the green pastures of what is now Kazakhstan. Known as Indricotherium, this gentle giant eventually became extinct.

On the walls of prehistoric caves, primitive paintings have been discovered depicting horses. These animals seem to closely resemble Przewalski's horse.

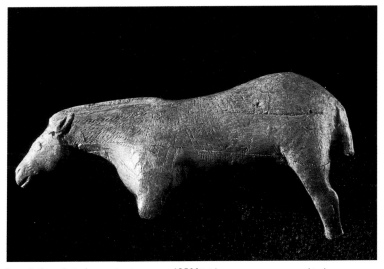

Long before their domestication around 3500 BC, horses were supposed to have mystical and even more gastronomic qualities.

The horse is known as a solidungulate: it has just one digit, remaining on each foot.

Just one digit...

With the onset of cold weather, the jungle gave way to temperate forest and then to wide open plains. The only means of survival available to an animal that was unable to defend itself were vigilance and speed. With its eyes placed on either side of its elongated head, *Mesohippus* had a panoramic view which enabled it to keep watch over a wide horizon. To increase its speed, the number of digits on each foot evolved to just three. This evolution continued in *Miohippus*

Grevy's, Burchell's and Mountain zebras can be distinguished by their individual markings. All can run at speeds of up to 65 kilometres per hour.

The stamina, spirit and placid nature of the ass were soon noticed by man and the domestication of this wild animal took place long before that of the horse. During the course of numerous exoduses and expeditions to conquer new lands, various crossbreeds were created such as the Poitou, the Puli and the Sicily. The cross between an ass and a horse is, without exception, a sterile animal. The mule is the result of a cross between a mare and a he-ass, whilst the hinny comes from a stallion and a she-ass.

All attempts at taming the zebra have failed.

and *Merychippus* with the outer two digits becoming smaller. These outer digits eventually became joined to the middle one forming the single 'canon bone' that is found in members of the Equidae family today. Over the years, these amazing anatomical developments have enabled each successive species to move more quickly.

Return to the homeland

Having evolved exclusively in America, the Equidae returned to the Old World at the end of the glacial periods, crossing the strip of land that at that time linked Siberia and Alaska. This migration continued until there were no Equidae left on American soil. Over in Asia, Europe and Africa, new species came about giving us the zebra, the ass...and the horse.

In search of lost Equidae

With its strange black and white striped coat, the zebra is the prime example of an Equidae that cannot be tamed. Today there are five subspecies of zebra, identifiable by their different coats. The stripes on the rump of each animal form a veritable set of fingerprints that are different in each individual zebra. Some have been hunted to extinction for the beauty of their skin, such as the quagga and Burchell's zebra which disappeared during the last century. Others have managed to survive in large African reserves. Wild asses have not had much more success. Forced out towards desert regions, the asses of Nubia and Somalia are gradually decreasing in number. In Asia, *Equus hemionus*, an ass with horse-like features, is also an endangered species; the chigetai is so rare that it is impossible to know its exact numbers and those of the onager of Persia, known as the khar in India, have also been severely reduced by the same diseases as those that affect the domestic horse. Over in Kazakhstan, the kulan became extinct in 1935. Only the kiang of Tibet, the largest of the ass family, has managed to survive more or less undisturbed due to the inaccessibility of its habitat.

From an early age, donkeys are strong and obedient.

The legend of wild horses

All horses are descended from either Przewalski's horse, the tarpan or the forest horse, the domestication of which began some 6000 years ago in Mesopotamia and China. The horses of today are the result of

Zebrules, zebrets and zebrids are the result of crossbreeding between zebras and other Equidae (donkeys and horses). All these hybrids are collectively known as 'zebroids'.

Many light horses that exist today, such as the Arab, share features with the tarpan, a wild horse which could still be found during the last century in the Steppes of eastern Europe. These rivals of the domestic horse were hunted in large numbers to the extent that in 1870, only one single mare remained. Fiercely shy, the animal refused to let itself be caught and inseminated and died on 25 December 1879. Since then, animals similar to the tarpan have been bred by crossing other wild breeds.

Only a handful of Przewalski's horses, discovered in 1879 by Nikolai Przewalski, still live in the wild in the grasslands of Western Mongolia.

Before they were reintroduced into the United States by the first colonizers, mustangs had not been seen on American soil for over 4 million years.

Proud American mustangs were imported from Spain.

crossbreeding and selection and have in effect been manufactured by man, losing many of their natural features in the process. Even the famous mustangs, those symbols of American freedom, are actually domestic horses that have been returned to the wild. In 1879, however, the original animal was rediscovered in the shape of Przewalski's horse. Unfortunately, by 1942 there were no more than a handful left. At the eleventh hour, four specimens were captured and sent to European zoos where they have since bred.

The term pony is not very old. It dates from the 17th century and has its roots in the Old French word 'poulenet', meaning 'little colt'.

Ponies and small horses

With a mocking look, laughing eyes and a large head crowned with a dishevelled mane, ponies frolic gaily, even in the rain, wind or snow. These lively kind animals are the much-loved companions of children and have retained many of the features of the horse of yesteryear.

The Welsh cob is a subspecies of the Welsh mountain pony, a Welsh breed through and through. This obedient pony is extremely good-natured and inexpensive to keep.

Of all the species native to the British Isles, the New Forest is the most varied. There is no one type and the height to the withers varies from 1.22 metres to 1.47 metres.

A ll early horses were small like the ponies of today. The latter have retained the sturdy stature of their ancestors, suited to the rigours of the natural environment in which they evolved. Still relatively numerous in the wild, they live in groups composed of a stallion, a mare and several foals. The pony usually measures no more than 1.48 metres to the withers, a feature which leads to significant morphological differences with other horses. Their relatively bulky body is longer than it is deep and is supported by four short legs. This unique

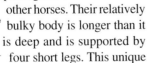

The Shetland brings its stocky build to any union with other breeds.

shape means that some Equidae measuring more than 1.48 metres to the withers are also classed as ponies.

The Shetland: small but strong

The Shetland pony is the smallest and oldest of the nine species of British pony. It is so old that its exact ancestry remains vague. One thing is sure, however. It hails from the Shetland Islands, 160 kilometres off the coast of Scotland, where it has lived at least since the Bronze Age (2000 BC). The animal measures around

The mane and tail of the Shetland pony protect it against bad weather.

The coat of the Shetland pony is usually black, but those with reddish-brown or chestnut coats are not uncommon.

one metre to the withers and is incredibly strong for its size.

The Highland: an all-rounder

Closely related to the Shetland pony, the Highland is considerably taller, measuring 1.47 metres to the withers. A descendant of the early ponies that inhabited northern Eurasia, and to which Przewalski's horse still bears a close resemblance, the original Highland was crossed in the 16th century with Percherons and Arabs, causing it to become slightly larger and more muscular whilst keeping its original shape. Resilient by nature, the Highland is, like its venerable ancestor, able to withstand the cold and is one of the few horses willing to carry the bodies of dead animals.

The Norwegian Fjord is probably related to the Highland.

The Exmoor: a waterproof Brit

The wild open spaces of south-east England have shaped the Exmoor. Considered to be the direct descendant of another primitive pony that was once found in north-west Europe, the Exmoor is a thoroughbred. It has evolved on its own, retaining many of the features of its prehistoric ancestors. It is quite small,

The Highland, an obedient and sure-footed pony, is ideal for children. Particularly suited to cross-country, it is not very fast but a keen jumper.

The Welsh mountain pony is regarded as the most handsome of British ponies and has given rise to three other Welsh species, including the Welsh cob. All have inherited its beautiful head with its large eyes and small pointed ears. The influence of light horses on ponies is clear to see, with many attributes coming from the Arab, the barb and the English Thoroughbred. The most famous Welsh mountain pony was a small thoroughbred called Merlin. Such was its fame that, in Wales, a pony is still referred to as a 'merlin'.

The Exmoor has a coat that protects it against bad weather.

reaching a maximum height of 1.3 metres to the withers, and powerful thanks to its hocks that are very close to the ground. Traces of a seventh molar, now non-existent in all other Equidae, are still found in its mouth. Its 'frog' eyes, fan-shaped tail and thick waterproof coat make it one of the most eccentric-looking ponies in the world: a real British character!

The Icelandic: a much-loved horse

Although not much bigger than the Exmoor, the Icelandic is

Having been threatened with extinction several times, the Dartmoor, an excellent competition pony, has been saved thanks to the determination of breeders.

The highly resilient Connemara is the only authentic Irish pony and is capable of surviving in areas where other Equidae would risk dying of hunger.

Eight hundred years in isolation have not diminished the qualities of the Icelandic.

considered to be a true horse on its island of origin. Like the Exmoor, to which it is closely related, this Equidae has retained a purity of gene thanks to a ban on the importing of horses into Iceland that was introduced in 930. At that time, disastrous attempts were made to cross Icelandics with oriental horses, all of which ended in failure. Today there are four types of Icelandic. Of these, the Faxafloi, from the south-west of the island – an area of high rainfall – bears a striking resemblance to the Exmoor, with the same solid muscular body as

The colour of the coat of a palomino must adhere to strict guidelines. It must have no markings and be similar in colour to a new gold coin.

Like the palomino, the pinto is a race that is defined by its colour since the size of individual horses can vary widely. Taken from Spain to America in the 16th century, the Spanish origins of these horses are reflected in their names. Palomino comes from palomilla, 'cream horse with white mane and tail', whilst pinto comes from pintado (painted). The coat, mane and tail of the pinto are two-tone. The white coat flecked with coloured markings is known as 'tobiano', whilst a coloured coat with white markings is called 'overo'.

The Haflinger has been bred in the Austrian Tyrol since 1945.

the latter. Furthermore, this little horse will eat almost anything.

The Haflinger: the pride of Austria

With its platinum blond mane and its smooth palomino or chestnut coat, the Haflinger is one of the most beautiful ponies in the world. This animal measures 1.4 metres to the withers and is mainly bred in the Tyrol mountains, a setting ideally suited to ensuring the continued sturdiness of the race. The genealogy of the Haflinger is worthy of royalty. The prestigious ancestor of all Haflingers is a half breed called El Bedavai XXII, the great-grandson of El Bedavai I, an Arab stallion imported to Austria-Hungary in the 19th century. Since then, nobility and simplicity have combined to produce a pony that can adapt to any environment and climate.

The Ariège and the Camargue: two prehistoric races

Pictures of the Ariège, with its beautiful black coat, were painted on the walls of caves by Cro-Magnon man, as were those of the white Camargue, originally from the Rhône Delta in southern France.

The sight of a herd of Camargues galloping through the marshlands of the Rhône Delta is an unforgettable experience.

The Ariège has developed a very sure footing from climbing the snow-covered slopes of the northern Pyrenees, a range of mountains in southern France.

The pottock (a Basque word) was a first-class smuggler.

The pottock: Basque and wild

The pottock, a pony from the Basque country, remained wild or semi-wild for many years. The three known types of pottock all share the feature of a concave area between the eyes. The two smallest breeds (the 'standard' and the 'piebald') measure between 1.14 metres and 1.32 metres to the withers, whilst the 'double' pottock can reach up to 1.47 metres.

The pottock, native to the Basque Country, has for many years been regarded as a wild or semi-wild pony.

 The Falabella: the Lilliputian of the horse world

Classed as a horse rather than a pony, the Falabella is the smallest of the Equidae. It is the result of the crossbreeding of small species (Shetlands and Thoroughbreds) and has a maximum height of 76 centimetres to the withers. The record for the smallest specimen is held by Sugar Dumpling, a mare from Virginia, that measured only 51 centimetres to its withers.

The Falabella pictured next to the shire, one of the largest draught horses.

The Caspian horse

Another small horse (less than 1.2 metres to the withers) is the Caspian. This horse was not discovered until 1965 by Louise l. Firouz, an American tourist to the area, who decided there and then to finance a stud farm in the region. It turned out to be the 'missing link' between the primitive horse of prehistoric times and the large horses that came from the desert.

The Falabella is a domestic horse that easily fits into any home!

Louise L. Firouz, who came across the Caspian horse whilst on a trip, bought several of these Equidae to create a stud farm in the area.

Regarded as the father of all other breeds of light horse, the Arab is one of the most beautiful of the Equidae family.

The Eastern ancestry of light horses

Thoroughbred and half-bred light horses, as well as other saddle horses, are all descended from two races from the desert: the Arab and the Barb. Characterized by long slender limbs, a narrow body and sloping shoulders, their shape is one of grace and speed.

The Arab thoroughbred is prized by the rich and famous of this world. In Morocco, palatial stalls house the most magnificent horses in the country.

With its mane and tail blowing in the wind, the Arab is the purest race of horse in existence. Its tremendous speed and straight back are sure signs of its racing ability.

All light horses are descended form the Arab thoroughbred, that legendary horse of the desert, originally from the Middle East. It in turn is descended from a wild Asian horse that galloped across the steppes and deserts some 7000 years ago.

The Arab: originally a warhorse

The Yemen is the country most frequently attributed with being the native land of the Arab. The

The tarpan from the deserts of central Asia is a distant ancestor of the Arab.

Bedouin selected the best specimens to create a fiery warhorse. After converting to Islam, these tribes kept precise records of the line of descent of their horses. The result of some fourteen centuries of breeding is the Oriental Arab, the most sought-after horse in the world of racing.

An exceptional horse

Thanks to its genetic qualities, this race has had an enormous influence on the world of horses in general. The Arab combines

The end of the Arab's muzzle is small enough to fit in one hand.

According to Bedouin legend, the horse Baz, owned by a descendant of Noah who lived 5000 years ago, is the original brood mare from which all other horses are descended.

The English Thoroughbred is the finest racehorse in the world. Thanks to highly selective and regulated breeding, it has managed to retain its exceptional qualities.

speed, stamina, strength and elegance. Its extraordinary talents, which are passed from one generation to the next, make it an exceptional horse. Although it is not very tall, measuring on average 1.5 metres to the withers, the Arab is never classed as a pony because of the shape of its body.

The prince of the racetrack

Its particularly long legs and rather short back (it has fewer ribs and lumbar and caudal vertebrae

After a pregnancy that lasts eleven months, the mare gives birth to a foal that is able to stand straightaway.

According to Muslim legend, God created the Arab in the image of the South Wind, placing a white mark on the forehead of the noble animal as a sign of glory and bliss.

The Arab thoroughbred has played an important role in the improvement of all species.

than other horses) are the obvious signs of a horse that can run fast. Furthermore, it has the distinctive feature of always having its tail raised, giving it a proud air like some dark handsome prince of the desert.

The Barb: the original North African

The Barb, another ancestor of all light horses, is a race native to the southern banks of the Mediterranean. Its exact origins

The English Thoroughbred, prized as a racehorse, is now bred all over the world, an indication of the economic importance of this species.

According to some theories, the ancestors of today's Barb survived the last ice age in a protected region, close to a fertile coast.

Lipizzaners have always been at the famous Spanish Riding School of Vienna.

are unknown but it is probably the descendent of an early European horse that migrated to North Africa. Like the Arab, it is a strong horse of the desert, but its physical appearance is different and it is reputed to have a more difficult character. During the 7th and 8th centuries, when the Arabs invaded North Africa, the Barb was crossed with the invaders' own horses. It has, however, kept its own particular characteristics, suggesting that it too has dominant genes that are passed from one generation to the next.

The Turkmen horse: running on empty

Another ancient race is the Turkmen horse whose origins are even more mysterious than those of the Arab or the Barb. Probably the descendent of a wild Asian race, it has a number of features in common with the Managhi, an Arab noted for its speed. The Turkmen has been bred for over three thousand years around the oases of the Turkmen Desert, on the south-east shores of the Caspian Sea. Famous for its stamina, this horse is capable of covering huge distances with only small reserves of water. In 1935, for example, Turkmen horses covered over four thousand kilometres in 84 days. Of this distance, almost a thousand kilometres were across the desert separating Moscow from Ashkhabad, one of the main breeding centres for these horses.

Eastern horses were spread throughout the world by the Arabs.

The English Thoroughbred: half Arab, half Barb

The English Thoroughbred, created in England during the 17th and 18th centuries, is the result of a cross between Arabs and Barbs. Three heads of Eastern families, the Darley Arabian, the Byerly Turk and the Godolphin

Originally bred in Turkmenistan, the Turkmen horse excels in competition: the stallion Absent won the gold medal for dressage at the 1960 Olympic Games in Rome.

▼ The Anglo-Arab, a cross between the English Thoroughbred and the Arab, must be at least one eighth Arab to be included in British studbooks which trace the pedigree of racehorses. In France, this figure rises to one fourth. These horses are usually the result of mating an English brood mare with an Arab stallion to produce a more slender animal. If they are the descendants of an Arab mare and an English stallion they are often not as valuable.

Large horses from small foals do grow! The bone below the knee of this foal will be over twenty centimetres long by the time it has finished growing at the age of three.

Suited to rodeos and cross-country, the quarter horse is also used by American cowboys to help round up their cattle.

The Anglo-Arab is mainly bred in southern France.

Barb, are in effect the founding fathers of this race. The breed of English Thoroughbred became established in the second half of the 18th century. At that time, the descendants of the three main families were crossed to obtain horses that were larger and faster than their ancestors, if slightly less hardy.

The quarter horse: an American sprinter

The quarter horse is the first wholly American race, bred in the colonies along the east coast of

The quarter horse is also known as the quarter miler since it was trained to run quarter mile races at high speed.

The Nez Percé, a North American Indian people of the Pacific coast, were the only Native American tribe to take a real interest in the breeding of horses. As far back as 18th century, this people produced the Appaloosa from horses imported and bred by the Spanish in the south-west of what was to become the United States. The main distinguishing feature of this horse, suited to racing and hunting, is its beautifully speckled coat. Furthermore, it has a white sclera (the area around the iris) and hooves that are both supple and strong.

The Andalusian, originally from Spain, was also one of the founding species.

the United States, mainly in Virginia. Trained to run quarter-mile races and round up cattle, this horse is extraordinarily muscular. The first Spanish horses brought to the United States at the start of the 17th century by the conquistadors (mixtures of Andalusian, Arab and Barb blood) were crossed with English Thoroughbreds to produce a race that oozes strength and speed.

The Waler: a strong-legged Australian

Descended from thoroughbreds (English and Arab), the Waler had to adapt to the harsh climate of New South Wales in Australia. These horses, which are now extinct, were used to carrying riders at high speed in the blazing heat. The Australian Waler, considered to be the best cavalry horse in the 19th century, was used in battles until World War I. The Waler's legs were both solid and agile. Being large (some horses measured as much as 1.63 metres to the withers), they were also good jumpers. In 1940, a Waler managed to clear 2.54 metres! It's successor, the Australian stockhorse, is said to have retained the same qualities, making it a good all-round horse.

The French saddle horse is the 'official' descendant of the Anglo-Norman; its stud book continues that of the Anglo-Norman.

H for Hanoverian

On racecourses the English Trotter is one of the most highly prized thoroughbreds.

Like most races known as 'saddle horses', the Hanoverian is a half-bred and is the most famous and widespread of its category. The race itself was first created in 1735 by George II, Elector of Hanover (Lower Saxony) and King of England, and is still highly sought after today. Some eight thousand mares are served each year by the athletic stallions of the Celle stud, a town in the north of Germany from where the Hanoverian originates.

The Hanoverian is a large athletic horse that can measure up to 1.68 metres to the withers. Its calm and obedient nature make it an excellent dressage horse.

The heavy-set Ardennes is recognizable by its straight head, square muzzle, protruding eyes and erect ears.

Draught horses

As well as domesticating the lighter saddle horse, man also found a use for the larger sturdier breeds that were perfectly suited to strenuous tasks. Known as draught horses, these large animals have all developed different characteristics according to the regions in which they were bred.

The Breton draught horse is a strong powerful animal that has been reared in Brittany (France) since the Middle Ages.

Given the name draught horses because of the way they are used to pull the appliances created by man, these large animals are characterized by a powerful chest, sturdy legs and large hooves, often covered with long hair known as fetlocks. Like their more slender cousin the saddle horse, they measure between 1.5 metres and 1.8 metres to the withers. The different races of draught horse are highly

In spite of its bulk, the Ardennes is amazingly nimble.

The Ardennes, noted for its calm placid nature, is often given to children to ride. But a word of warning to all stallions with one thing on their mind: the females will need some wooing!

The green pastures of the Ardennes in France and Belgium provide the ideal setting for the rearing of foals and their subsequent growth into magnificent draught horses.

The lighter Ardennes are used for riding in the forest.

varied but are all the progeny of more or less ancient breeds.

The Ardennes: the Methuselah of draught horses

The Ardennes is without a doubt one of the oldest breeds of draught horse. With its incredible square muzzle, it has many features that recall those proud prehistoric horses of which it is probably one of the last direct descendants. Prized since ancient times for its unparalleled stamina and strength, the

Ardennes was almost certainly used as a charger in the Middle Ages. The harsh winters of the region in which it was bred, the Ardennes in France, have contributed significantly to its legendary sturdiness.

The Belgian

'Of all the peoples of Gaul, the Belgians are the bravest.' These words from Caesar refer to the inhabitants of Belgium but could have equally applied to the courageous horse that had the good fortune to please him. Known in the Middle Ages as the Great Horse of Flanders, it gradually adopted the name of its most famous country of origin. The animal is enormous. Its short squat back, stocky legs and impressive strength have led it to be crossed with other European breeds of draught horse, such as the heavy Italian draught, the English shire and the Irish draught.

The shire: the colossus of draught horses

As far as sturdiness is concerned, the shire, originally from the English Fens, is as equally impressive as its ancestor, the Belgian. Measuring 1.8 metres to

The Poitevin is a familiar sight in the marshlands of the Poitou and Vendée.

With their long thick fetlocks, imposing stature and hard muscular limbs, the draught horses of the North are among the sturdier species.

▼ The Poitou ass is a large species (1.6 metres to the withers) that is extremely strong. Crossed with the Poitevin, a powerful Nordic draught horse that was introduced into France to drain marshland, this ass gave birth to a sturdy mule known as the Poitou. Famous for its strength and longevity, the latter is able to withstand the harshest of conditions. Having for many years been prized as a draught animal in the European countryside, it went on to become the trusted friend of the brave American pioneer.

The Comtois, closely related to the Ardennes, is a light draught horse often put to work in the forests and vineyards of eastern France.

Weighing in at over a tonne, the shire is one of the largest horses in the world.

the withers and weighing in at 1200 kilograms of pure muscle, the shire is the largest of all horses. Its strength is extraordinary and two shires can easily pull a cart weighting 18 tonnes! Everything about this horse's physique is adapted to such tasks: incredible muscles, exceptionally large hooves and a highly developed neck.

The Boulonnais: the dandy of draught horses

The Boulonnais, a horse from the north of France, is one of the

The Suffolk punch is the oldest race of British draught horse, once set to work ploughing the heavy soils of Suffolk in England.

most elegant draught horses. Its graceful form is the result of distant crossbreeding with proud Arab steeds. The first crosses date back to around 50 BC when horses from North Africa were used by Julius Caesar in his campaigns in the north of Gaul.

The Percheron: a mixed-blooded beauty

Originally from the Perche region in Normandy, the

Sturdy draught horses have no problem surviving harsh winters.

Arab horses captured during the Crusades were crossed with the Boulonnais to produce a graceful physique that is exceptional among draught horses.

The coat of the Percheron is most often dappled grey or black, but other colours are also possible, such as bay bordering on reddish-brown.

Percheron too owes its beauty to the presence of Arab blood. Its roots go back to the Battle of Poitiers. In 732, the stallions abandoned by the routed Saracens mated with heavy French mares. The fruits of these 'mixed marriages' were then raised in the green fields of the Perche where the mild humid climate, the lush grass and a subsoil rich in lime and phosphates combined to produce a horse that is today sturdy, strong and majestic.

The Percheron is an excellent specimen for the purposes of crossbreeding.

Horses in Our World

The horse was an integral part of the great campaigns of the Middle Ages. Those heavy enough to carry the weight of a knight in armour were known as chargers.

Warhorses

In the days of old, the advantages of having horses in battle were clear: soldiers on horseback or carried in horse-drawn chariots easily had the edge over soldiers on foot. The nomadic tribes of the central Asian Steppes were masters of the art of fighting on horseback and have inspired generations of horsemen.

The election of Abraham Lincoln, a fierce opponent of slavery, to the US Presidency in 1860 signalled the start of the Civil War in which the cavalry played an important role.

As soon as the horse was domesticated, it was used to fight. In the third millennium BC, the horse was already an important part of the lives of the nomadic tribes living in the Steppes of Eurasia. It was bred and trained to accompany families in their expeditions across the vast plains. As the herds increased in size, the nomads extended their territory, taking over new land more often than not using force during the course of bloody raids.

In the 7th century BC, Assyrian archers ruled the Orient.

A horse civilisation

The Scythians, heirs of the first nomadic horsemen and originally from the area north of the Black Sea, spread terror throughout the powerful Persian Empire from the 8th to the 4th centuries BC. They travelled as far as Syria, and even threatened the all-powerful Egyptian Empire. Their technique: archers on horseback harried and terrorized isolated villages, pillaging them and then galloping away. Ten centuries later, the terrible Huns, under Attila, left their mark on Europe using the same technique. The grass trampled beneath the hooves of their horses would never grow again.

In the vast steppes of central Asia, horses provided the best means of covering large distances and conquering new lands.

It is impossible to talk about Alexander the Great (356—323 BC), one of the most powerful military leaders of ancient times, without mentioning his favourite steed, Bucephalus, which carried him to numerous victories. Its name, meaning 'ox head', was chosen because of the horse's large forehead, a sign of eastern ancestry. Bucephalus was so spirited that no one was able to mount him. Noticing that Bucephalus was afraid of his own shadow, Alexander turned him to face the sun and jumped on his back.

Greek horses: too small to be ridden

Whilst they lived at the same time as the Scythians, the first Greeks used horses differently. In the 8th century BC, Greek warriors went into battle on chariots pulled by horses. Once at the battle ground, the warriors fought on foot since their horses were not strong enough to carry them. Four centuries later, the Greeks decided to try their hand at horse-riding, importing hundreds of Scythian mares.

Greek chariots were also used as a mode of transport by members of the nobility.

The Assyrians' horses were impressively reared and trained. They were carefully selected following procedures that are not dissimilar to those still used today.

Roman chariots were used in circus games, or, as shown here, as part of military processions organised to celebrate a general's victory.

Horses made and broke the Roman Empire

The Romans kept horses for use by their army, as a backup for the infantry. In 54 BC, the conquest of Britain was a success largely due to the intervention of the cavalry. At that time, soldiers charged their enemy holding a lance under one arm. Five centuries later, the horse also played a part in the fall of the Roman Empire, harried first by Goth horsemen and then by the Huns.

Long ago in Japan, the formidable samurai warriors also fought on horseback.

The horsemen of Islam

Having discovered the horse in the 4th century, the Arabs soon became masters in the breeding and training of these animals. In the Koran, the noble beast is credited with bringing good luck and prosperity. Imbued with these qualities, it became the driving force of the Holy Wars. With horsemen as an integral part of their battle plan, 8th-century Arabs conquered the Iberian Peninsula as far as the Great Wall of China.

During their conquests, the Arabs relied heavily on the fiery nature of their horses.

Like the Muslims who fought in their jihad, every Christian knight took part in the Crusades, fighting in the name of their God and King to win back the Holy Land.

In the 17th century, the enormous stables of the sultan Moulay Ismaïl in Meknès, Morocco, held almost 12,000 horses.

At the beginning of the 13th century, Genghis Khan founded the Mongol empire, conquering the northern part of China, Afghanistan and eastern Iran on horseback.

From a very early age, the noble knights of the Middle Ages were trained in combat. Not to slay some terrible dragon, but to wipe out their enemies. Whilst still young, these knights became outstanding horsemen, able to brandish a lance or sword in one hand whilst holding the reins and a shield in the other. Like its master, the steed was protected by solid armour and was also trained in combat. It was able to intimidate the enemy by kicking out and spinning round in order to protect itself.

The arrival of chargers

In the West during the Middle Ages, new breeds were created in order to produce stronger horses capable of carrying the weight of knights in their armour. Chargers – so called because they were ridden at speed at the enemy – filled the battle fields of the age. In peacetime, knights fought each other during tournaments, simulating future combats.

Even the chargers wore armour, such was the ferocity of the battles.

Classic horsemanship

The heavy chargers of the Middle Ages eventually gave way to lighter breeds that enjoyed a golden period in military history from the 17th to the 19th centuries. Throughout the world, horses and horsemen fought for the glory of their country. The invention of firearms did little to change the way in which wars were fought and heroes still rode into battle with 'swords drawn'. For this reason, man was not the only one to pay a heavy price for victory – and defeat. In 1812, during the Russian campaign, France lost 50,000 horses. In America, the horse played an important part in the conquest of the West and in the fight for independence. The

In 1429, aged just 17, Joan of Arc headed the small army that forced the English to lift their siege of Orleans.

American Civil War (1861–1865) was finally won by the North that had a larger cavalry than the armies of the South.

The Great War tolls the death knell for the cavalry

The last battles in which horses were used on the front line were those of the Great War. The large nations taking part in the conflict still had their cavalries, a hangover from the previous century, but in Europe, the mud

The Russian retreat marked the end of the road for thousands of men and horses.

Thousands of horses also died during the Crimean War. Each battle was an inferno punctuated by the deafening sound of hooves.

During World War I, horses were used mainly away from the front to move canons and injured soldiers, rather than in the battles themselves.

 of the fields and trenches prevented them from being used. Through lack of care, however, over a million horses still perished at the front without even taking part in the fighting. Now replaced on the battlefield by lorries and armour-plated tanks, the horses of today's armies are used to portray a particular image of the military during parades and processions, displaying their mastery of all aspects of dressage.

In Paris, a parade of the famous Republican guardsmen.

The Horse Guards, the cavalry section of the British sovereign's Household Brigade, are changed twice a day. They have been protecting the British sovereign since 1660.

With a long tradition that dates back to the golden days of the European royal courts, dressage still conjures up a certain image of nobility as portrayed by this horseman.

Dressage: the pinnacle of horsemanship

For the cognoscenti, dressage is a highly-developed art form in which man and horse skilfully perform a number of set pieces. This noble discipline was once part of a classical tradition reserved for the elite but is now taught in a number of prestigious riding schools to which many a rider aspires.

Dressage has existed for centuries and is now a popular discipline. Riders in the equestrian theatre of Zingaro are constantly updating the classical figures of the haute école.

In the magnificent setting of the Hofburg Palace, the Spanish Riding School of Vienna put on innovative displays which retain all the spirit and perfection of the classical discipline.

D ressage is a popular equestrian sport and the ultimate symbol of sophistication, discipline and elegance. With its roots firmly in classical, aristocratic and military tradition, few are the riders who reach the highest level in this discipline.

The haute école

The object of dressage is to teach riders to master their mount completely by developing the horse's

The horsemen of the Cadre Noir are masters of the 'courbette'.

physical and mental qualities through a strict training programme. The goal is a union in which rider and mount become one. Their bodies fuse together to recreate the mythical creature of the centaur. 'Campagne' teaches the rider the art of performing a series of fixed exercises whilst retaining a natural 'air'. The 'haute école' (high school) is based on even stricter rules: focussing on 'collection' – in which balance is moved towards the rear of the horse –

The uniform of the riders of Vienna consists of a two-pointed hat and a tobacco-coloured jacket with tails.

As far back as the 16th century, Japanese trainers used the rope and post technique when initiating their proud mounts into the finer points of the equestrian art.

Only three types of jump are permitted in the performances of the Vienna school: the 'levade', the 'courbette' and the 'capriole', performed here with panache.

Ever since ancient times, circuses and acrobats have demonstrated the talents of exceptional riders and horses. Even if masters of the 'haute école' have tended to look down on their acrobatics, there is no denying the talent of men such as Philip Astley, James Fillis and François Baucher who introduced classical moves into the circus ring in the 18th and 19th centuries. More recently, the Grüss family circuses and the amazing equestrian theatre of Zingaro have continued the tradition of dressage as a form of entertainment.

At the Royal School of Jerez, riders pass between the posts during the salute.

the rider makes his mount perform a number stylized moves with mathematical precision. Classical steps such as the 'piaffe' and the 'passage' precede jumps, such as the 'courbette', the 'croupade' and the 'capriole'. These moves are often set to music with rider and partner performing a skilful dance. When this choreography is performed by a group of horses – known as a 'reprise' – the result is a veritable equestrian ballet. The principle of the 'haute école' is to achieve absolute perfection in the execution of these moves and in the presentation of the rider and horse, all judged according to strict technical and aesthetic criteria. Combining tradition, purity and beauty, dressage transforms horseriding into a veritable art form.

A noble passion

It all began in Naples back in 1532 when Frederico Grisone founded the first riding school. It proved an overnight success and young European nobles flocked to his academy to learn the finer points of dressage. Many of the techniques were inspired by those of the

Byzantine cavalry who advocated the use of the bit, saddle and stirrups and had already performed the 'piaffe' and the 'passage' several centuries earlier. Ideas contained in the first known work on equestrianism and the science of dressage written by the Greek Xenophon (355 BC) lead to further modifications.

The discipline of dressage

During the 16th century, people relied on brut force to train horses. Whips

Bits and harnesses have evolved over the centuries.

The saddle room of the Spanish Riding School is certainly one of the best-stocked in the world. Royal saddles similar to those used during the 18th century are still made here.

Pillar work is an important part of classical dressage. Invented by Pluvinel, this technique is vital in training horses to perform the 'levade' and the 'rassembler'.

The Andalusian tradition of dressage was copied throughout Europe.

were used all the time and the animal was often fitted with a bit covered with large spikes. Stubborn horses were made to move by tying a burning torch or a live cat or hedgehog to their tails. The century was heavily influenced by the ideas of Descartes and the horse was regarded as a piece of precision machinery that had to be ruled with a rod of iron. Soon, however, man realised that horses could be trained without resorting to such barbaric methods. Famous names such

At Jerez de la Frontera in Spain, the tradition of the Andalusian school dates back to the 15th century when the monks refused to cross their thoroughbreds with other races.

In the 16th and 17th centuries, Antoine de Pluvinel, an important figure in the history of dressage, taught Louis XIII to master all the finer points of this refined art.

as Pluvinel, Cavendish and La Guérinière played an important part in rehabilitating the noble animal without using coercive methods.

Riding masters

As equerry to the King of France, Pluvinel was an important figure at the court of Louis XIII. It was he who invented the technique of using pillars between which horses had to weave in and out. This method, still used in the most prestigious riding schools,

Another type of dressage is performed at the Moscow Circus...

schools, teaches the horse raised airs. In 1730, La Guérinière, the director of the Tuileries royal riding school in France, introduced new attitudes that were later to be adopted by the schools of Vienna and Saumur.

Vienna and Saumur: the Meccas of equestrian art

The tradition of the Spanish Riding School of Vienna dates back to the end of the 16th century and the reign of the Habsburgs. Influenced by La Guérinière's writings on dressage, the school has taught the airs performed at the height of Versailles' fame for almost four centuries. The school owes its Spanish title to the origin of the horses admitted to its stables: Spanish jennets and Lipizzaners. Another academy of world renown is the national riding school of Cadre Noir at Saumur in France where riding has been taught in the pure French tradition since 1825. Displays by the Cadre Noir and the Vienna school have introduced the art to a growing public and since the 1912 games in Stockholm, dressage has been an Olympic discipline

Dressage competitions have become an prestigious Olympic discipline.

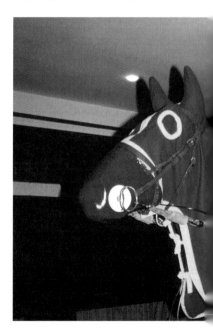

Only white Lipizzaner stallions are allowed in the prestigious stud farm of the Vienna school. Traditionally, however, there is always one bay specimen.

Whilst it is true that training in the 'haute école' is a long procedure for horses, beginning in their first year, riders too are also subjected to an arduous programme. It takes between four and six years before they are allowed to ride the finest animals and even then, the first 'levades' and 'caprioles' often leave new recruits with some memorable bruises. For this reason, the school of Cadre Noir has recently acquired a robot named 'Persival' that is able to simulate moves on computer.

The gauchos are the cowboys of South America who round up cattle in the pampas of Argentina.

Willing beasts of burden

Long after its domestication, the horse was finally used to help man in his work. Having taken the place of the ox in the countryside, it then became a feature of the large towns of the industrial revolution. In turn, however, it was forced to give up its place to another type of horse – 'horsepower'.

Horses are still quite commonly used in forests for carrying tree trunks and branches. They are more environmentally friendly than tractors and are cheaper to run.

Workhorses were a rare sight in the Middle Ages.

After 4000 years of being used for mainly warlike ends, the horse was eventually employed in more peaceful activities. It was not until the 18th century, however, that man's 'proudest conquest' took over altogether from the ox as a draught animal. At that time, farming techniques were changing and new machines were being invented that were ideally suited to the regular speed of horses.

In some parts of the world, horses are still used to bring in the harvest but this tradition has increasingly become a thing of the past.

AroundValencia in Spain, a number of horses, well adapted to the dry climate of southern Spain, are still kept to work the land.

The ass is another animal that can carry heavy loads without tiring.

An asset for the rural population

By 1860, the horse was an essential part of farming. Seven million of them were already working in the fields of America. By the eve of World War I, that number had risen to twenty five million, used to pull combine harvesters and other enormous pieces of machinery. Twenty five years later, with the invention of the tractor, most horses were put into retirement.

Post haste

The non-violent use of horses focused on the animal's natural qualities, namely the ability to cover large distances in a short time. The horse-drawn carriages of Europe and the stagecoaches of the United States were most popular during the 18th and 19th centuries. In often difficult conditions, passengers were subjected to a trying journey, broken by frequent stops at coaching inns where the horses were changed. Whilst post was once carried at the same time as passengers, a specific postal service was established in Britain as early as the end of the 17th century. The example of the British mail coach spread throughout the rest of Europe and eventually reached the New World. It was in America that the legendary Pony Express was established, transporting post across Indian territories between Missouri and California. Each rider was relayed every 100 kilometres. The journey, which was carried out at a gallop, made it necessary for each rider to change horse every 15 kilometres. In ten days, 3000 kilo-

The riders of the *Pony Express* had to be prepared for any situation.

Day and night, mail was carried by horses across country, sometimes at the same time as passengers. To ensure a rapid service, the horses were regularly changed.

In 1828, some fifty years before the electrification of tramways, a regular service of public transport pulled by powerful horses was introduced in Nantes, France. Known as 'omnibuses', since these horse-drawn vehicles were for use by all, this method of transport soon spread to all the major cities of Europe. London, Paris and Berlin were the capitals in which the largest number of horses were used. In the 1870s, the General Omnibus Company of London had over 22,000 horses.

metres were covered at great risk to the lives of the riders and horses.

A 'galloping' industry

Paradoxically, it was during the industrial revolution that the workhorse had its moment of glory. Far from being replaced by machinery, draught horses proved to be effective partners in industry from the 19th to the beginning of the

Blinkers prevent the horse from seeing sideways so that it does not become distracted.

Whilst the horses used at the turn of the century were not as fast as the engines of today, they were nevertheless able to reach the scene of a fire quickly.

In the 18th century, a strong horse was able to tow a barge carrying a 60-tonne load.

Pit horses had to pull a fixed number of trucks each day.

20th century. In all areas, horses were of assistance to man: on the railways, they pulled trains full of goods while in factories, they powered the machinery. In the darkness of iron and coal mines, they pulled convoys of wagons until the day they died without ever having seen daylight. Along canal banks, they were charged with pulling heavy barges full of goods over distances of several dozen kilometres.

The rural exodus of the horse

In the 19th century, most working horses were to be found in towns and cities. Raised in the green pastures of the countryside, they were brought to work in the bustling roads and streets. Strong black horses pulled hearses whilst others drew fire engines. The cleaning of streets, delivery of coal, ferrying of passengers in

The funeral of the victims of an airship disaster in France, 1909.

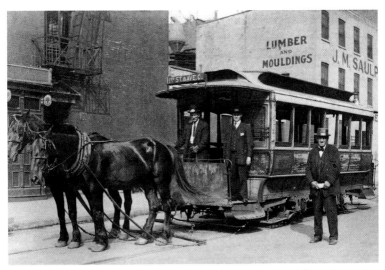

During the last century, trams, like omnibuses, were pulled by powerful heavy horses. In spite of their stamina, their lives were never very long.

Journeys by stagecoach were long and uncomfortable for the travellers. They were often held up and the passengers robbed by Indians and highwaymen.

Although much fewer in number than during the 19th century, horses are still put to work in cities and towns. Most are today used by the police.

calashes or omnibuses, transport of goods – everything was done by horses. In 1900, a city like New York had around 175,000 horses whilst those in Paris numbered over 100,000. Worn out by constant hard work, their life expectancy was dramatically reduced and these zealous servants more often than not finished up on the butcher's slab in France, or in the stomachs of cats and dogs in Britain and America.

In Prague, horse-drawn carriages take you back in time.

The handsome creature pulling this elegant carriage is a far cry from the pitiful sight of those 19th century teams of horses, exhausted by overwork.

Throughout the world, horses have proved a useful addition to many police forces, commanding respect by their sheer strength and impressive stature.

In 1994, five pottocks were bought by a French hydro-electric company looking after some 18 damns on the Rhône River. These small semi-wild horses that will eat anything in their way were set free on an area of land owned by the company by way of an experiment to see if they could be used as natural weedkillers. On this occasion, the pottocks successfully replaced poisonous weedkillers and expensive equipment. And at the same time, they got revenge on modern machinery on behalf of all horses!

Forest horses...

Today, workhorses have been replaced by the combustion engine and are largely a thing of the past. In some countries, however, these faithful servants are experiencing something of a revival. More than just a simple trend, the use of horses in German and Swiss forests is becoming more and more widespread and is beginning to replace some mechanical equipment. Able to navigate winding paths more easily than tractors, these powerful horses weave smoothly in and out of obstacles without crushing the bark or damaging the roots of the wood they are carrying.

For forest work, the horse more than adequately replaces any four-wheel drive.

...and police horses

Similarly, in some towns and cities horses continue to work, this time in the police force. In Canada, the famous mounted police still patrol on horseback, a tradition repeated in most large cities such as New York and London. During riots and demonstrations, the imposing size of the horse commands the crowd's respect and enables the rider to have a clear view of the situation.

The strength and stamina of the horse have made it a popular choice of animal in all types of sport, particularly in racing and crazy competitions such as the one pictured above.

Horses in sport

Throughout the world, horses have for many centuries been prized as playmates. Admired for their bravery, strength and especially their speed, they have always proved willing participants. Today, they have become the stars of the racetrack and are the mainstay of a booming industry.

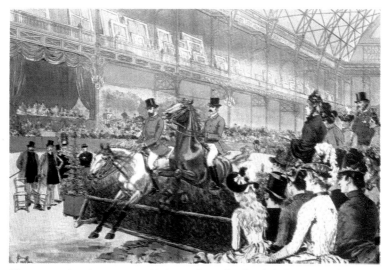

Horse racing has always attracted followers from all walks of life. Back in the 19th century, top hats and delicate veils rubbed shoulders with less formal attire.

Horses have taken part in sporting events for several thousand years. The first major competitions in the West began in Rome, one century before the birth of Christ.

A Roman gamble

Approaching the first hairpin bend at speed, the chariots send up a cloud of dust as they move dangerously close together. The teams of horses, panting and covered with sweat, are whipped to spur them on. One team is

Chariot racing: a popular circus game back in ancient Rome.

The circus games of ancient Rome have become immortalized in the film *Ben Hur* in which Charlton Heston takes part in an epic chariot race.

The architecture of the arena took on cosmic dimensions: the central obelisk represented the sun whilst the twelve gates stood for the constellations of the zodiac.

thrown off balance and ends up spread across the track. Stunned, the crowd hold their breath then let out loud cries and whistles of joy and excitement... Such was the spectacle enjoyed almost everyday and free of charge by some 385,000 Romans who watched the races of the Circus Maximus, the largest arena in the whole of Ancient Rome. Heralded by trumpets, the chariot race was the highlight of the festivities and a pretext for some lively betting. The stakes were high and accidents frequent. Both men and horses

The excitement is building when suddenly a chariot topples over on the track...

could lose their lives on the oval track, or go on to win fortunes as the champions. The image of Ben Hur is one that lives on.

The kings of the arena

Bulls were also a feature of the circus games of Ancient Rome but were fought on foot. Much later, on the Iberian Peninsula, men began bullfighting on horseback. Today, bulls are still fought in the noble Lusitanian tradition with men criss-crossing the ring on horseback without killing the bull. In the Spanish corrida, only picadors and rejoneadors get to ride on large decorated mounts form where they can face the charging bull without being exposed to its horns.

On July 2 and August 15, the Italian city of Sienna becomes the setting for the 'Palio'.

Polo: an Asian sport!

Polo, the epitome of British chic, was first played in Persia over 2000 years ago. For many years, the sport was popular in China, Japan and India, where Her Majesty's subjects discovered it in the 19th century. Imported into the United Kingdom along with tea, the sport was originally called 'horse hockey' and soon became a sport enjoyed by the

Bullfighting on horseback continues today in Portugal whilst in Spain, the corrida has taken place on foot since the 18th century, with only the picadors entering the ring on horseback.

Hunting is without a doubt the oldest sport to be carried out on horseback. In France, it is the stag and the wild boar that are hunted. In England, they prefer to hunt foxes, whilst in Australia it is the wallaby. In order to take part, riders must pay a fee to the 'Master of the Hunt'. As soon as the dogs have scented the prey, they set off after it at top speed, barking to signal their position. Following behind, only the most skilled horsemen arrive in time to put the exhausted animal out of its misery.

In an explosion of colour and sound, the 'Fantasia' of Morocco is a lively demonstration of equestrian and military superiority.

upper classes, often played at garden parties where the ladies had the chance to show off their amazing hats.

Traditions and pastimes

The horsemen of central Asia and North Africa spent most of their lives and free time on horseback. In the Mongolian steppes, races combining speed and endurance were reserved for adolescents who rode bareback over long distances, covering over 50 kilometres at a

From India to the United Kingdom, polo is a sport enjoyed by the upper classes.

Originally played by the gauchos of the pampas, polo has become a national sport in Argentina. Introduced to the game in 1877, it is now the breeding ground of champions.

gallop. In the Afghan game of Bozkashi, the are no holds barred as the participants fight over the remains of a goat. In North Africa celebrations, horses covered with jewels and coloured materials jostle with each other amidst the noise of shouting and gunshots.

Ride 'em, cowboy!

The rodeo was officially founded with the Wild West Show on July 4, 1866 in Arizona. The programme of events included

In Mongolia, children take part in the race to celebrate the festival of Naadam.

Originally from Afghanistan, the game of Bozkashi, during which participants fight on horseback over a dead goat, has been adopted by other tribes of horsemen, such as the Mongols.

As part of the American rodeo, steer wrangling is a colourful event celebrating the hard lives of those cowboys who played an important part in conquering the Wild West.

a carnival, a shooting competition, chariot racing and, last but not least, a sport inspired by the competitions held between cowboys on their return to the corral. This event consisted of four disciplines: the lassoing of a calf, the riding of a wild bull, and, to finish, two attempts at riding broncos (wild horses), one bareback, the other with a saddle. A classic of Wild West culture.

Accomplished sportsmen

In a number of equestrian disciplines, riders and their

You need a sturdy pair of jeans to ride the bucking bronco!

Jappeloup, the king of jumping... Of the many horses that take part in international competitions, some names remained etched on the memory for ever.

The thoroughbreds that take part in horseraces are all descended from three Arab stallions: the Byerly Turk, the Godolphin Barb and the Darley Arabian. The latter was promised as a present by Sheik Mirza to the consul Thomas Darley. When the Sheik failed to keep his promise, Darley went ahead and took the horse, angering the Arab dignitary who wrote to Queen Anne, 'my stallion, stolen by certain of your subjects, was worth more than a king's ransom'. Today, the frozen sperm of a prized racehorse is worth millions.

mounts are regarded as top level sportsmen. Show-jumping, with its circuit of walls and fences, is reserved for jumpers. Three-day eventing, an Olympic sport consisting of dressage, cross-country and showjumping, is the most prestigious of all the disciplines whilst harness racing is also a very popular sport.

Cross-country, the most spectacular part of three-day eventing, has its dangers.

They're under starter's orders

For thousands of years, the Chinese, Mongols, Greeks and Romans have placed bets on horseraces. In Europe, the foundation of the British Jockey Club in 1752 helped to formalize the running of races. Racecourses became larger, reflecting the expectations of a public that dreamed of winning a fortune. Flat racing, steeplechase and harness racing are all major sources of betting and are controlled in France and America by the Pari Mutuel. In Britain, informed forecasting is the domain of the bookmaker. Jockeys and Thoroughbreds stand to become famous whilst their owners and trainers can become extremely rich.

Men do not have a monopoly on equestrian heroism: mythical women, such as the Valkyries of Nordic legend, have also excelled on horseback.

Myths and stories about horses

In legend, even the most spirited horse eventually finds a master who tames it and rides it during amazing exploits in which mount and rider become inseparable. It is often impossible to choose between the heroic acts of man and beast, such is their partnership. In Ancient Greek mythology, their appearances combine to form the creature known as the centaur.

According to various different myths, Apollo, the Greek god of light, drove his solar chariot across the skies. He seems to have been a very impulsive god...

The Western (here, Clint Eastwood's 1985 film *Pale Rider*) glorifies the last remaining myth surrounding the horse, inseparable from the Indians, cowboys, bandits, gold prospectors, missionaries...

S itting proudly astride his mount, man becomes a hero among men. Ever since ancient times, when horses were used by warriors, the animal has fascinated people and has become closely associated with the exploits of both men and gods.

The spirited horses of the Sun

Helios, the Greek god of the Sun, drove his chariot across the sky each day, tracing the path of this the most important of

The horsemen in the film *Urga* cross the steppes of Mongolia at a gallop.

stars. The reins of these celestial horses, however, were not for novices! Phaëthon, the son of Helios, disobeyed his father and borrowed the solar chariot. Unfortunately, the inexperienced boy lost control of the divine vehicle which dived towards the Earth. Zeus, in order to prevent a catastrophe befalling all those on Earth, struck down the young man with a thunderbolt. It is said that ever since, Helios has wept every night over the death of his son and that his tears fall to Earth and form the morning dew.

Chiron, the wise centaur, taught Achilles the secrets of medicine.

The Amazons, the race of women warriors of Greek mythology, may actually have existed in Russia, not far from the Kazakh border.

Hidden inside a large wooden horse, the Greeks, led by Odysseus, succeeded in entering the city of Troy.

Pegasus: the horse of the skies

Another mythical horse from Ancient Greece is Pegasus, the winged horse and secret son of the Gorgon Medusa, a terrifying creature who transformed anyone who looked at her into stone, and of the god of the sea, Poseidon. Pegasus escaped from the body of his mother when she was decapitated by the hero Perseus, the son of Zeus. The wild winged horse was tamed by a great warrior, Bellerophon, who aimed

The Greek hero Bellerophon astride Pegasus managed to kill Chimera, the terrifying monster with the head of a lion, body of a ram and tail of a snake.

to ride it to Olympus. Zeus, however, had other plans and unseated the vain rider who was badly injured in the fall. His winged mount faired somewhat better since Zeus, aware of its outstanding qualities, transformed it into a constellation.

The centaur: half man, half horse

The centaurs were fantastic immortal creatures with the head and torso of a man on the body of a horse. They were born from the illicit affair between Ixion and

The centaurs, the epitome of all that is vain, represent the animality of war.

Magnificent is the name of the horse that carries Beauty, the heroine of the 1946 film *Beauty and the Beast* from the home of her father to the castle of the Beast.

It is not surprising that the eight-legged Sleipnir was chosen as the swift mount of Odin, the supreme creator god of the Vikings.

Rosinante, the horse of Don Quixote, is as tall and skinny as her master.

Hera, the wife of Zeus. Like their father, who was condemned to hell by a jealous Zeus, the centaurs were arrogant, proud and boastful. Chiron was the only centaur to escape this dreadful inheritance. Charged with the education of Achilles and Jason, he also played the role of mediator in the conflicts which set his brothers against Hercules. Accidentally hit by a poisoned arrow fired by the hero of twelve labours, the wise Chiron, with the agreement of the gods, transferred his immortality to Prometheus in order to end his terrible suffering.

Between heaven and hell

According to northern European mythology, the Valkyries, a Nordic legend based on the Amazons, rode across the battlefields looking for dead heroes who were worthy of being taken to Valhalla, the paradise of the immortal. In a different vein, the four horsemen of the Apocalypse (Victory, War, Judgement and Death) inspired many religious artists during the Middle Ages.

The horse: a better friend to man than his own wife!

According to one North American legend, the spirit of the West wind made a man and a woman (Atam and Im) from its warm breath. At the same time, a wicked gnome created a white horse to play tricks on them. The spirit of the West wind warned the couple about the horses powerful kicks. In addition, he gave the horse a tail and a mane to ward off the flies that the gnome was sending to torment it. The spirit of the West wind then ordered the horse to serve man. Seeing that his wicked plan had failed, the gnome suggested that the couple try the sacred fruit that at that time grew on pine trees.

The sound of horses' hooves herald the arrival of the Valkyries...

Apocalypse, the last book of the Bible and attributed to Saint John, describes the four horsemen representing Victory, War, Judgement and Death.

The unicorn, a mythical white horse, had a single horn in the middle of its forehead. The only way to entice the creature out of hiding was to sit a naked virgin under a tree. Fascinated by the young woman's beauty, the unicorn allowed itself to be captured. The horn of the unicorn was believed to offer a universal cure for poisoning and attracted the interest of royal families. Queen Elizabeth I paid a hundred thousand pounds for one of these horns even though sceptics today claim that it was nothing more than the tusk of a narwhal.

Jolly Jumper, the travel companion of Morris' cartoon character Lucky Luke, is by far the most intelligent horse in the West...and indeed the world!

In North America, the Native Americans managed to overcome their fear of the horses left to roam wild by the fleeing Spanish conquistadors.

Tornado, Zorro's faithful mount, cuts through the night like a bolt of lightning.

Although the spirit of the West wind had forbidden them to touch this delicious fruit in his absence, the woman allowed herself to be tempted by the gnome, tasting the forbidden fruit and sharing it with her husband. In a flash, all the fruit turned into pine cones, dry and inedible. The spirit of the West wind flew into a terrible rage. He forced the disobedient woman to spend the rest of her life with the gnome and made another partner for the man out of one of his ribs.

HORSES

around the world

North America

Atlantic Ocean

* The famous mustang, introduced by the Spaniards, later returned to the wilderness.

South America

Pacific Ocean

Arctic

* Przewalski's wild horse is the last true wild horse of our planet.

Europe

Asia

* Japanese like to watch races between workhorses.

*Wild
sses still
oam the
Sahara.

Africa

* The Arab thoroughbred is the ancestor of all present-day race horses.

Indian Ocean

Australia

 ponies and small horses

light horses and thoroughbreds

work horses

wild equidae

Antarctic

HORSES

Principal Species

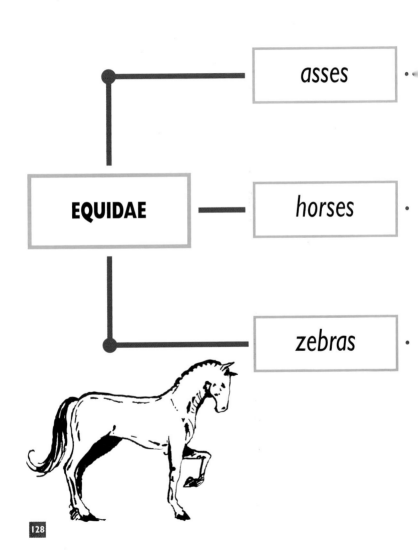

EQUIDAE

asses

horses

zebras

Equus asinus is certainly the most robust. Asses were domesticated in early times, but still survive in the wild.

The pony is a short-legged horse who can be mounted easily even by small children.

Light horses are famous for their speed. They have successfully maintained the hot temper of their desert-inhabiting ancestors.

Workhorses greatly contributed to alleviate human toil. They have been mostly used for transport and in agriculture.

Roaming in the African savannah, the untameable zebra shows off his unique coat.

In our days, Przewalski's wild horse, the last of its kind to survive undomesticated, is mostly found in zoos.

Creative workshop

Having studied all of these creatures,
it's time to get creative.

All you need are a few odds and ends and a
little ingenuity, and you can incorporate
some of the animals we've seen into
beautiful craft objects.

These simple projects will give you further
insight into the animal kingdom presented in
the pages of this book.

An original and simple way to enjoy
the wonderful images of the animal kingdom.

The horse. A decorative frame

*T*hese *two proud archers on horseback, executed in correction fluid, have come from the Orient to adorn a frame for your loveliest souvenirs.*

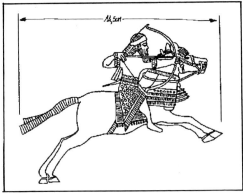

Photocopy the pattern and blow it up to the desired size, then trace it.

Drawing the horses

• Take the correcting pen and practise drawing straight lines and curves on the glass to get used to

handling it. The line should not be broken or uneven. To prevent this, press evenly on the cartridge inside the barrel of the correcting pen to get an even flow of white.

• Place the pattern under the glass, centred towards the top, and fix it to the reverse side with the adhesive. Copy the design as it shows through the glass.

• Then move the pattern to the bottom of the frame and turn it over to face the other way; copy as before.

Decorating the frame

• Make a frieze 0.5 cm from the edge of the frame, following the

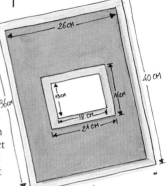

pattern. Then place two waves beneath the top horse's hooves and another two waves behind the rider at the bottom.

Fixing the paper

• Glue your three sheets of paper one on top of another, keeping them all centred. Stick the photograph 13 x 18 cm onto the central sheet and put the glass and the back support together, keeping the side on which you have drawn facing towards the paper.

Materials

For a photograph
13 x 18 cm:
• A glass mount
measuring 30 x 40 cm
• Three sheets of
coloured paper,
one 30 x 40 cm,
one 26 x 36 cm and
one 16 x 21 cm
• A spray-can of glue
• A white correcting
pen • Adhesive
• A sheet of tracing
paper

Horse brooch

*W*ith its mane flowing in the wind, this beautiful golden horse brooch set off with golden beads will add sheen and sparkle to any outfit.

Photocopy the pattern and blow it up to the desired size.

than the pattern.

Cutting and baking

Preparing the modelling clay

• Knead the modelling clay until it is soft and easy to handle, then roll it out on the sheet of glass using the rubber roller like a rolling pin until you have a slab about 3 mm thick and a little larger

Place the photocopy on the slab of Fimo and press it down lightly with the palm of the hand so that it stays firmly in place. Cut through the sheet of paper and the modelling clay with the cutter at the same time.

• Remove the excess all round, leaving only the shape of the horse. If the edges are not straight, pat them smooth with the flat of the cutter blade. Place the horse on a

sheet of aluminium foil and put it in the oven at 130°C for 25 minutes.

Painting

• When the horse is completely cool, paint it with the can of gold spray paint and tap the powdered pigment onto it with the paintbrush (particularly on the horse's back).

Use the tweezers to stick the golden beads onto the horse's back, mane, tail and hooves. Stick on the blue bead

for the eye.
• When it is dry, fix everything with the lacquer spray or fixative (to hold the pigment in place).
Turn the horse over and stick the brooch mounting onto the back with the glue.

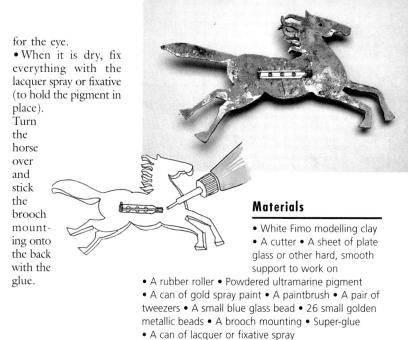

Materials

• White Fimo modelling clay
• A cutter • A sheet of plate glass or other hard, smooth support to work on
• A rubber roller • Powdered ultramarine pigment
• A can of gold spray paint • A paintbrush • A pair of tweezers • A small blue glass bead • 26 small golden metallic beads • A brooch mounting • Super-glue
• A can of lacquer or fixative spray

Domino box

*A**n antique-look stylised horse on a two-coloured box of dominoes.*

Preparation

Photocopy the design, adjusting its size to fit that of your box.
• Using the awl, make

the lid for a handle.
• Brush a coat of gesso all over the outside of the box (taking care not to paint any inside

a hole in the lid through the notch that you use to open it. So that you will still be able to close the box after adding your new handle, make a notch in the wood of the box of the same size as the object that will be placed on

the groove in which the lid slides, nor on the runner edges of the lid itself, as the slightest thickness would stop the lid from closing). When the coating is completely dry, sand it down lightly with sandpaper to obtain a smooth support on which to paint.

Painting the background

• Paint the inside of the box and the underside of the lid black. Allow to dry.
• Then paint a good

half of the outside of the box and of the upper side of the lid with white paint into which you have mixed a hint of yellow to obtain an ivory colour. Allow to dry.
• Cover half the box, including the short sides, and half the lid with the adhesive film. Paint the uncovered parts in brown: one long side and half of the short sides, and half the lid. Allow to dry. Remove the adhesive slowly so as not to pull off the paint underneath.

Painting the horse

- Go over the reverse side of the photocopy with a lead pencil leaving a broad line ; place on the upper side of the lid and

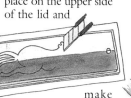

make a transfer.
- Stick adhesive film on the lid and cut out the film pressing very lightly, following the line of the transfer and taking care not to cut the paint and the wood at the same time.
- Apply black paint with the fine-tipped paintbrush inside the shape you have cut out. Allow to dry thoroughly before removing the film.

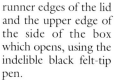

Finishing
- Colour the two runner edges of the lid and the upper edge of the side of the box which opens, using the indelible black felt-tip pen.
- Take the item to be used as a handle; place and then glue it into the hole made for the purpose.

Materials

- A deal box • Acrylic paint in black, white, brown and yellow
- Acrylic ground or gesso • An awl • A cutter • A medium brush
- A fine-tipped paintbrush • Super-glue • 1A piece of shell, or some braid and a piece of driftwood, or a cupboard handle or any other object of your choice which can serve as a decorative handle • Adhesive tape • Transparent adhesive film
- Spray varnish • Fine sandpaper • A lead pencil • An indelible black felt-tip pen

Horse picture

*T*he plaster used to make this little picture may not be the most usual material, but it will give your mischievous colt another dimension by allowing you to make it in relief.

Trace the shape of the horse onto the cardboard.

Putting on the plaster

• Then begin placing small pieces of plaster bandage on top to give relief to the shape. Dip the pieces

in water one at a time and place them on the shape as required.

• When the horse has been built up in relief, cover the rest of the picture with wider strips. Cover the edges of the frame too, and fold the strips back behind the board. Allow to dry for 24 hours.

Painting

• Then paint the background in blue acrylic and the horse in white. Paint little grey flecks on the horse to give it a dappled effect.

The mane, tail and hooves are black.

Don't forget to paint round the edge to frame your picture.

Drive a little hook into the cardboard so that you can hang your picture on the wall.

This technique can be used for any other design of your choice.

Materials

• Tracing paper • A piece of fairly thick cardboard, roughly 21 x 30 cm
• Acrylic paints

Photographic credits

AKG: 11a, 13a, 61, 76, 79b, 83, 86a, 103, 104a, 105a, 105b, 107a, 106-107, 114, 121b, 122a, 122-123, 123a, 125a; Cameraphoto: 115.
CAT'S COLLECTION: 104b, 116a, 116b, 118, 120b, 124, 125b.
COSMOS: Buthaud: 108a; Sibert: 110a, 112-113.
D.R.: 9a, 117b, 119a.
EXPLORER: 85a, 109; ADPC: 62; 68a, 69; Bertrand: 110b; Jean-Louis Charmet: 92-93; Mary Evans: 92, 97; coll Es: 95b; FPG International: 96b; Hurlin: 112a; coll Maciet: 95a; Nou J.-L.: 37b; Tetrel P.: 117a; Varin: 113a.
GAMMA: 111a; Andreini: 106a; Bernstein Keith/Spooner: 33a; Brissaud-Gellie 78a ; Freiss 80a; FSP/Jones Ian: 32b; Kingfisher: 82a; Kubasci: 102; Lehr 85b; Le Toquin 79a, 82b, 87a; Novosti: 43a; Petit 78b; Ruitz-Treal: 35, 68a, 69; Sallaz: 111b; Stevens: 42a; Vandeville 84a, 81a, 84b ; Voge 80-81.
GALLOU: 86-87.
GARDE RÉPUBLICAINE: 74b.
JACANA: Axel: 47a; Jacques Brun: 51; Cauchoix Denis: 16a, 32a; Champroux Jean-Pierre: 27a; Sylvain Cordier: 30, 36a, 36b, 90b; Dressler: 6, 8b, 10a, 126b ; Durandal: 28a, 46-47; Eckart Pott Dr: 27b; Ch. Errath: 54; Gallais: 14-15, 129a ; Felix Guy: 48; Frederic: 20, 108b, 129b ; Leeson: 2, 131; Lemoine Elizabeth: 6, 41b; Lichter: 19b, 126a ; Mero: 24-25, 28-29, 37a, 40a, 40b, 101, 127a ; Moiton C&M: 24a; Paul Nief: 56a; Rainon Alain: 38; Ph. Rocher: 91a; Schwind Herbert: 22b, 23b; Jean-Paul Thomas: 5, 58a; Guy Thouvenin: 54-55; Guy Trouillet: 55; Varin/Visage: 41a, 52a ; Veiller Henri: 49a, 53b, 89; Wegner Jorg & Petra: 29a; Wiesniewski: 4; Wild 14a.
KINGFISHER: 8a, 10-11, 12a, 13b, 19a, 33b, 64, 65, 64-65, 66a, 66b, 67a, 67b, 68b, 70a, 71a, 70-71, 73a, 73b, 74a, 88, 90a, 91b, 93, 94a, 119b, 120a, 121a.
NATURE/CHAUMETON: 5, 45b, 50, 52b, 53a, 58b, 59a, 59b, 126c, 127c, 129d ; Bending: 34; Boris: 31a; Colibri/Dubois: 7, 127b; Ferrero: 21,22a, 23a, 25a, 26b, 31b, 39a, 39b, 44, 45a, 46a, 49b, 56b, 57, 129c; Gohier: 100-101; Hellio: 42-43; King: 129f; Lanceau: 16-17, 18, 26a, 129e;
Polking: 15a; Reille: 17a.
ROGER VIOLLET: 12b, Branger: 60; ND: 94b; 96a.
ZINGARO/POUPEL: 77.

Front cover
Jacana, Mero
D. R. (A)
Kingfisher (B)

Back cover
Nature/Chaumeton, Ferrero(A)
Kingfisher (B)
Jacana, Rainon Alain (C)
Kingfisher (D)

Acknowledgements:

The publishers would like to thank all those who have contributed to this book,
in particular:
Guy-Claude Agboton, Antoine Caron, Jean-Jacques Carreras, Michèle Forest,
Céline Gerst, Rizlane Lazrak, Nicolas Lemaire, Hervé Levano, Marie-Bénédicte Majoral,
Kha Luan Pham, Vincent Pompougnac, Marie-Laure Sers-Besson, Emmanuèle Zumstein

Illustration: Frantz Rey

Translation: Kate Clayton - Ros Schwartz Translations, Michael Mayor

Impression: Eurolitho - Milan
Dépôt légal: September 1998
Printed in Italy